# poles apart

## Life at the Ends of the Earth

*wild dog*

## by Dr. Mark Norman

Polar Bears live in the Arctic at the top of the world...

Polar Bears and penguins don't live together. In the wild, they would never even meet.

# North Pole

…while most penguins live in or near Antarctica at the bottom of the world.

The Arctic and Antarctica are similar places at opposite ends of the Earth — they are both very cold with lots of snow and ice. Winters are dark, and in summer the sun shines twenty-four hours a day.

# South Pole

3

# North Pole

The Arctic is an ocean surrounded by land. If you stand at the North Pole at the very top of the Earth, you would be on frozen sea ice over deep ocean. The sea floor would be two-and-a-half miles below you.

Antarctica is land about the same size as North America, and is surrounded by sea. It is covered by a fat layer of ice known as the **Ice Cap.**

If you stand at the South Pole at the bottom of the Earth, you would have to dig through almost two miles of ice before you reach solid rock.

**South Pole**

5

# North Pole

Many plants live in the Arctic. They need to be small, tough plants that can survive being squashed under heavy snow each winter. In summer the ice melts and the plants bloom. These plants form a region known as the **tundra**.

The Snow Hare is one of the many animals that feed on the plants of the tundra.

It is so cold and dry in Antarctica that very few plants can survive here. There is not a single tree in all of Antarctica — the nearest tree is over 600 miles away! The only plants that can survive here are mosses and tough lichen. Only tiny mites can feed on these plants.

# South Pole

The Arctic is connected to North America and Russia, so many insects arrive overland every summer. Other insects have eggs or cocoons that can survive through the winter. In summer the tundra is buzzing with butterflies, moths, beetles, dragonflies, and swarms of mosquitoes.

Only a few tough bugs can survive in Antarctica. There is not much to eat on land and they can't fly anywhere to escape the winter. Some of the flies on Antarctic islands have even given up flying and lost their wings — they are called 'walks'.

## South Pole

Puffins are like the penguins of the Arctic. Like penguins they are great swimmers — but unlike penguins, puffins can fly.

Some puffins even have similar strange hairdos to crested penguins.

Penguins are only found on the bottom half of the world. Their little wings are useless for flying but are excellent for steering when swimming.

South Pole

The top **predators** of the Arctic are the Polar Bears. When hunting over the ice, a Polar Bear will sometimes hide its black nose with its paw so that it can blend into the snow. This makes it easier for the large creature to creep up on sleeping seals. A Polar Bear is a great swimmer, and will eat everything, from roots and berries to hares and seals.

One of the top predators of the Antarctic is the Leopard Seal. It hunts like a crocodile, cruising around in the water with only its eyes and nostrils sticking up out of the water as it looks for penguins to eat.

South Pole

The Arctic landscape changes from plants and tundra in the summer, to a frozen world of snow and ice in winter. Hunters like the Snowy Owl and Arctic Fox turn white in winter to blend in with the snow.

In Antarctica, it is cold enough for snow and ice all year round. White is a good color for **camouflage**, so many birds like Giant Petrels stay white all year.

## South Pole

Some types of seals like to cuddle together to keep warm. Walruses have to be careful not to poke their neighbor in the eye with their tusks! They use their tusks to climb onto floating ice. Males will also use their tusks to fight.

In Antarctica, Elephant Seals also like to cuddle. Pups grow fat on oily milk, then pile together to stay warm.

The pups have to stay out of the sea until they are big enough to swim faster than their main predators, the Killer Whales.

## South Pole

Some seals in the Arctic like to party. Bearded Seals sing songs under the ice — early explorers thought they were mermaids singing!

Male Hooded Seals have rubbery noses that they can blow up to look like red balloons. They do this to attract a mate.

Like humans, seals are air-breathers. Weddell Seals dive under the Antarctic ice to hunt for fish and octopus. They breathe through a hole in the ice, which they keep open by scraping back and forth with their front teeth.

# South Pole

One of the strangest animals of the Arctic is the Narwhal. These whales have only two teeth. Males grow one of these teeth to a six-foot-long tusk that sticks out of the front of their heads. Males use their tusks to spar, just like a sword fight.

Minke Whales are the most common whales in Antarctica. They search along the edges of the sea ice for schools of tiny shrimp known as Antarctic **krill**.

These whales feed by gulping big mouthfuls of water and krill. Then they squirt the water out through a sieve of special hairy plates in their mouths, called **baleen** plates, trapping the shrimp.

# South Pole

Winters are hard at the ends of the
Earth. In the Arctic, all the plants are
buried under snow and ice.
Muskoxen have thick fur and huddle
together for warmth. They dig through
shallow snow to get to the
frozen grass underneath.

In Antarctica, male Emperor Penguins have the toughest winter. They spend months in the freezing dark, shuffling around with an egg on their feet.

Males won't eat for about a hundred days while they wait for their female mates to return in spring with food for the new chicks.

# South Pole

As the sun returns in spring, the snow melts in the Arctic and the tundra plants are uncovered. Animals return to feed and have their young.

Caribou walk and swim across lakes while birds flock from everywhere. Wolves and Red Foxes arrive to hunt.

In springtime in Antarctica, the sea ice melts and tiny krill form huge swarms. Seabirds fly south and whales swim from warmer waters to feast on the krill. Male Sperm Whales arrive to hunt for big squid.

## South Pole

People have lived in the Arctic for more than 5000 years.

The **Inuit** (*in-you-it*) live in the Arctic across northern Russia, North America, and Greenland. In northern Europe, the Sami people are the traditional herders of reindeer.

There is no land connecting Antarctica to other countries, so this frozen continent was only discovered by explorers about 200 years ago.

Today the only people who live here are scientists doing research into wildlife, weather and **global warming**.

# South Pole

Global warming is already affecting these special places at the ends of the Earth. In both the Arctic and Antarctic, the snow and ice is melting more and more each summer. **Glaciers** are getting smaller, and animals like Polar Bears and penguins need our help.

There are many things you can do today to help protect the wildlife of the Arctic and Antarctic, such as:

- plant trees wherever you can
- walk, ride or use public transport
- reuse things and make them last longer
- fix broken things; don't throw them away
- buy locally made things, not products shipped or flown around the world
- recycle everything you can
- buy less stuff
- join a conservation group
- write to your politicians to see what they are doing and ask how you can help
- turn off the air-conditioning and open the windows
- get your school to plant trees and buy eco-friendly things
- do research and find out more!

# GLOSSARY:

**baleen:** numerous flat plates made of modified hair in the mouths of some whales, used to strain krill and plankton from seawater.

**camouflage:** the natural coloring or form of an animal which enables it to blend in with its surroundings.

**global warming:** the warming of the Earth caused by the release of carbon dioxide into the atmosphere, mainly from the use of fossil fuels and the clearing of forests.

**Ice Cap:** a permanent covering of ice over a large area, especially on the polar region of a planet.

**Inuit:** the indigenous people of Greenland, northern Canada, Alaska, and north-east Siberia.

**glacier:** a slowly moving mass of ice formed by the build-up and compaction of snow on mountains or near the poles.

**krill:** tiny, shrimp-like animals, which are the main source of food for penguins and baleen whales.

**predator:** an animal that hunts and eats other animals.

**prey:** an animal that is hunted or eaten by another animal.

**tundra:** a vast, flat Arctic region of Europe, Asia and North America in which the subsoil is permanently frozen.

# INDEX:

Join the millions of people around the world who are changing the way they live to tackle global warming:
Greenpeace: www.greenpeace.org
World Wide Fund for Nature:
www.panda.org
www.wwf.org
Al Gore Climate Change campaign: www.algore.com

This edition published in 2010 by

**wild dog books**

15 Gertrude Street
Fitzroy Vic 3065
Australia
+ 61 3 9419 9406
+ 61 3 9419 1214 (fax)
dog@bdb.com.au

**wild dog books** is an imprint of black dog books

Designed by Ektavo Pty Ltd
Printed and bound in China by Everbest Printing International Pty Ltd

Distributed in the U.S.A. by
Scholastic Inc.
New York, NY 10012

ISBN: 9781742031590 (pbk.)

10 9 8 7 6 5 4 3 2 1          10 11 12 13 14 15

IMAGE CREDITS:
Shutterstock: front cover, pp i, 2, 3, 4, 5, 6, 8, 9, 10, 11, 12, 13, 14, 16, 24, 31, back cover;
istockphoto: front cover; Grant Dixon / Hedgehog House: p. 7; Colin Monteath /
Hedgehog House: p. 13; Tui De Roy / Hedgehog House: p. 15; Mark Carwardine /
Hedgehog House: p. 21; Bryan and Cherry Alexander / Hedgehog House: p. 26;
Dr Roger Kirkwood: pp 9, 23, back cover; Photolibrary: pp 11, 16, 18, 19, 22, 25;
Dr Mark Norman: pp 27, 31; Paul Nicklen / National Geographic: p. 20